Animals
in Winter

Animals in Winter

by Susanne Riha

Carolrhoda Books, Inc./Minneapolis

This edition first published 1989 by Carolrhoda Books, Inc.
Original edition copyright © 1987 by Annette Betz Verlag im
Verlag Carl Ueberreuter, Vienna and Munich, under the title
WIR SCHLAFEN BIS DER FRÜHLING KOMMT.
All English-language rights reserved by Carolrhoda Books, Inc.
Additional text copyright © 1989 by Carolrhoda Books, Inc.
Printed in Austria and bound in the United States of America.

Library of Congress Cataloging-in-Publication Data

Riha, Susanne.
Animals in winter.

Translation of: Wir schlafen bis der Frühling kommt.
Summary: Describes what various animals do to prepare
for winter. Includes the marmot, bat, squirrel,
hamster, butterfly, and others.
1. Animals—Wintering. 2. Juvenile literature.
[1. Animals—Wintering. 2. Winter] I. Title.
QL753.R5713 1989   591.54′3   88-18876
ISBN 0-87614-355-9 (lib. bdg.)

ANIMALS IN WINTER

During the winter, many animals find sheltered spots and hide themselves away. Inside these burrows and holes, they enter a sleeplike state called **hibernation**. Their breathing and heartbeat slow down, and their temperatures fall. While they are hibernating, animals usually do not need food. They can live off the fat stored in their bodies.

If the outside temperature rises during winter, many hibernating animals may wake up from their sleep. They may even leave their hiding places and go out into the snow-covered world. When winter cold returns, they go back to their warm burrows to wait for spring.

The animals included in this book live in a part of Europe where winters are cold. Their habits are very much like those of North American animals that live in a similar climate. In the back of the book, you will find a list of American animals that spend the winter hibernating, like their European relatives.

MARMOT

The young marmot climbs onto a tree stump in the middle of the mountain meadow. He makes a shrill, whistling sound and listens for an answer. Where are his brothers and sisters? The little marmot does not like being alone on this fine autumn day.

After crossing the mountain stream, the marmot sees two of his brothers. There they are, sleeping in the sun. He waddles over to join them, and soon a friendly fight starts. Squeaking and squealing, the young marmots push and bite each other. They end their play by rolling down a grassy slope together.

But be careful! The owl is watching from her perch in a hollow tree. The young marmots run and hide in their burrow among the rocks. This burrow is their summer home, where they were born and where they live with their parents.

Soon, the members of the marmot family will be moving to their winter burrow. In preparation, they will bring grass to line the den, which is deep underground. Then, when the cold comes, the marmots will go into their shelter, along with other members of their family. They will block the tunnel leading to the den with rocks and dirt. As snow falls on the mountains, the marmots will huddle together and begin their winter sleep.

Scientific name: *Marmota marmota*
Body length: 2 feet (60 cm)
Weight: 9 to 18 pounds (4 to 8 kg)
Food: Plants, grass, roots
Lifespan: 5 to 6 years

GARDEN SNAIL

The leaves have changed color, and the sky is gray. The garden snail's year is coming to a close.

In the spring, the snail spent most of her time in the damp, shadowy forest. She crept over the forest floor on the flat "foot" that she extended from her shell. Mucus produced by a gland in her foot made a slippery path over which she could glide. The forest was full of plant food for the snail to eat. With her filelike tongue, she scraped off pieces of tender leaves. On some dark nights, the snail would make a short trip to the farmer's vegetable garden for a tasty salad of lettuce leaves.

During the summer, the garden snail mated with another snail. About a month later, she laid many small, round eggs in a hole she had dug in the ground. After covering the hole with dirt, the snail left the little eggs to develop on their own.

On hot summer days, the snail found a place in the shade and stayed inside her shell. She waited for rain to bring the moisture so important to her life.

Now winter is coming with its cold and snow. The snail digs down into the loose soil and goes inside her shell. She seals its opening with a hard chalky cover. Protected in this shelter, she will wait for the first warm rains of spring.

Scientific name: *Helix pomatia*
Shell diameter: 1½ inches (4 cm)
Food: Plant parts
Lifespan: 2 to 3 years

EUROPEAN BADGER

The badger sticks his head out of his burrow on the edge of the forest. The air is cold, and snow may be on the way. It is almost time for the badger's winter rest.

He has already prepared for the cold months to come. During the long nights of summer, he ate himself fat on berries, mushrooms, and bird eggs. He gathered grass to line his burrow, collecting large bundles between his chin and front legs. Moving backward, the badger dragged these bundles through an entrance tunnel of his underground home. The badger's burrow is so large and has so many tunnels that he shares it with another animal. A fox has made a home in part of the burrow.

As the sun sets on this autumn day, the badger decides that winter is not quite here. He can see some young badgers playing in the meadow. Their mother has not yet taken them into her burrow for the winter. Time for one more hunt. Perhaps the badger can find a beehive with some delicious honey or honeycomb. His thick fur will protect him from the bees' angry stings.

Scientific name: *Meles meles*
Body length: Up to 3¼ feet (1 m)
Weight: 44 pounds (20 kg)
Food: Berries, mushrooms, roots, snails,
        worms, frogs, field mice
Lifespan: Over 12 years

HAZEL MOUSE

Under the full autumn moon, the two hazel mice are harvesting blackberries. Quickly, they move from branch to branch, picking and eating the juicy berries.

The little mice are plump because they have been eating steadily for weeks. Last night, they feasted on acorns. Tomorrow, they may go after hazelnuts. Sweet hazelnuts are the favorite food of hazel mice and the reason they were given their name. (Hazel mice are also known as common dormice.) They like hazelnuts so much that they break open the shells and eat the nuts right off the branch.

These two hazel mice, like all their relatives, are very much at home in the branches of trees or bushes. They had their babies in a round nest of grass and leaves built in a birch tree in the woods. That was in the spring. Now the young hazel mice are almost as big as their parents and ready to go off on their own.

Soon all the hazel mice will have to leave the trees and find a shelter underground. In burrows lined with grass and leaves, they will pull their tails up over their heads and sleep until spring.

Scientific name: *Muscardinus avellanarius*
Body length: 3½ inches (9 cm)
Tail length: 2¾ inches (7 cm)
Weight: 1 ounce (30 g)
Food: Fruits, berries, hazelnuts, acorns, insects
Lifespan: 3 years

COMMON EUROPEAN FROG

It is November. The water in the pond has begun to freeze. Along the shores, the reeds are dead and dry. How different everything looks from the time in spring when the frog first came to the pond.

In spring, the frog was attracted to the pond by the croaking of male frogs. After mating with a male, she laid hundreds of eggs in the water. About a week later, tiny tadpoles hatched from the eggs. Many of the tadpoles were eaten by fish or water beetles, but some survived to develop into adult frogs. When the young frogs left the pond, their tails were all that remained of their lives as tadpoles.

After laying her eggs, the female frog had gone off on her own. She spent the summer looking for food in and around the pond. Little fish, snails, and worms were included in her diet. She particularly liked insects, which she caught on the end of her long, sticky tongue.

Now the frog has come back to the pond to prepare for winter. She must find a shelter to protect her from the cold. Perhaps she will hide under a pile of dead leaves. Or she might bury herself in the soft mud near the shore. Hidden from sight, she will wait for spring.

Scientific name: *Rana temporaria*
Body length: 4 inches (10 cm)
Food: Snails, worms, insects, little fish, tadpoles
Lifespan: 6 years

MOUSE-EARED BAT

On this moonlit autumn night, the mouse-eared bat flies out of the attic in the old house. She flutters over the fields and the dark woods, stopping to rest on a steep, rocky wall. Swooping over a pond, she takes a drink of water. As she flies, she catches and eats insects.

To find her way in the night, the bat does not use her eyes. She depends on her hearing for a guide. While she flies, the bat makes a sound so high that humans cannot hear it. The sound bounces off objects in her path and comes back to her large ears as echoes. By listening to these echoes, the bat can avoid bumping into things. The echoes also tell her where to find insects.

When the bat left the attic tonight, a young bat came with her. The youngster is her three-month-old baby. Born naked and blind, the young bat spent its first weeks clinging to its mother's body. Now it is strong enough to fly and to hunt its own food. After a night of hunting, the two bats may spend the day sleeping in a hollow tree.

In a few weeks, the bats will have to find a better shelter. Winter is on its way, and bats need to be protected from the cold. Mother and young will go to a cave where the air is damp and still. Hanging by their strong claws, the bats will wrap their long wings around their bodies and begin their winter sleep.

Scientific name: *Myotis myotis*
Body length: 2⅓ inches (6 cm)
Wingspan: About 1 foot (35 cm)
Weight: ¾ ounce (25 g)
Food: Insects
Lifespan: 2 years

HEDGEHOG

The hedgehog is in his winter shelter under the roots of a big tree. He is curled up beneath the leaves and straw. Perhaps he is dreaming a hedgehog dream of spring.

When the warmth of the spring sun wakes him, he will be very thin and hungry. The hedgehog will set out to find food—insects, snails, snakes, and earthworms. He will swim streams and even climb fences to get a meal. When he reaches the top of a fence, he rolls up in a ball and drops off on the other side. His spines make a cushion for his fall.

In the spring, the hedgehog may return to the farm where he spent some time last year. Perhaps the people at the farm will put out dog biscuits and water for him again. If the farm dog tries to grab him, the hedgehog will roll himself into a prickly ball.

Spring will also be the time for mating. To get a mate, the hedgehog may have to fight with other male hedgehogs. One spring day, his mate will give birth to five or six baby hedgehogs with short white spines. Three weeks after their birth, the little hedgehogs will have the same sharp, spiny armor as their parents.

Spring will be a busy season for the hedgehog. But now it is winter, and time for rest and dreams.

Scientific name: *Erinaceus europaeus*
Body length: 11 inches (30 cm)
Weight: 1½ pounds (700 g)
Food: Insects, snakes, mice, chicken eggs, mushrooms, roots
Lifespan: 5 years

RED SQUIRREL

On this bright winter day, the red squirrel has left her nest in the woods because she is very hungry. She finds a pinecone and quickly eats the seeds hidden under the scales. But this is not enough to satisfy her. Hidden somewhere in a hollow tree stump, she has a supply of nuts and seeds. The squirrel sets out to search for her storehouse.

The woods are covered with snow now, but during the summer, the red squirrel collected mushrooms here. In the spring, she built a round nest of twigs, grass, and bird feathers in a pine tree. Here is where her three babies were born. Tiny and hairless at first, they gradually developed fluffy tails and tufts of hair on their ears, like their parents. By midsummer, they were old enough to leave the nest.

The red squirrel crosses the ice-covered stream in which she bathed in summer. There is the birch tree where she once found a bird's nest full of tasty eggs. In autumn, she gathered chestnuts from those tall trees in the park. But where is the tree stump?

Finally, she sees it in a clearing in the woods. Dashing over the crusty snow, the red squirrel reaches her food supply. After helping herself to some nuts and seeds, she returns to her nest for another winter nap.

Scientific name: *Sciurus vulgaris*
Body length: 10 inches (25 cm)
Tail length: 8 inches (20 cm)
Weight: 10½ ounces (300 g)
Food: Nuts, berries, seeds, mushrooms, bird eggs, young birds
Lifespan: 12 years

FAT DORMOUSE

It is bitterly cold outside. The sun is pale in the winter sky. Inside his burrow in the hollow tree, the fat dormouse is deep in hibernation. He will probably not stir until spring.

When spring comes, the dormouse will have a lot to do. As soon as he wakes up, he will clean himself from head to toe. He will be very hungry after the long winter, so at twilight, he will go to look for food. Moving quickly among the trees, the dormouse will search for bird eggs, insects, and berries.

After his hunger is satisfied, the dormouse must decide where to make his summer home. Should he join the other dormice living in the old barn? Perhaps it would be better to build a nest in a tree. If he makes a nest, he could collect building materials from the attic of the farm house. He would have to be careful not to make too much noise, or the people in the house might hear him.

As he goes about his springtime jobs, the dormouse will have to watch out for the pine marten. This member of the weasel family likes dormice for dinner. If the dormouse sees a marten, he will hide himself in a rock crevice.

But now the dormouse does not have to worry about hungry pine martens. Hidden in his hollow tree, he is still wrapped in a deep winter sleep.

Scientific name: *Glis glis*
Body length: 7½ inches (19 cm)
Tail length: 6 inches (15 cm)
Weight: 3½ ounces (100 g)
Food: Fruits, berries, nuts, acorns, insects, bird eggs, young birds
Lifespan: 3 years

EUROPEAN BROWN BEAR

The brown bear has awakened in the middle of winter. It is a mild day, and she has left her den to wander on the snow-covered mountain slopes.

The bear is spending this winter alone, but for the last two years, she had company in her den. Two winters ago, she gave birth to two cubs. The baby bears were as small as rabbits, and their eyes were tightly closed. All that winter, the mother bear stayed in the den with her cubs, feeding them her nourishing milk.

In the spring, the cubs were old enough to leave the den. During the summer, they followed their mother as she went looking for food. By watching her, the little bears learned what things were good to eat. They learned how to catch fish in the stream and to get eggs from an ant nest. One of their favorite foods was the sweet honeycomb that they found in beehives in hollow trees. When they were not busy exploring, the cubs played with each other. They wrestled and tumbled on the grass while their mother kept close watch.

During the following winter, the brown bear and her two cubs shared a den. By summer, the young bears were almost grown, and their mother sent them off on their own. This winter, the female bear is alone, but it will not be long before she starts a new family.

Scientific name: *Ursus arctos*
Body length: Up to 10 feet (3 m)
Weight: Up to 1,750 pounds (800 kg)
Food: Fish, rodents, ant eggs, berries,
      fruits, mushrooms, honeycomb
Lifespan: Up to 30 years

EUROPEAN HAMSTER

There is still a lot of snow on the ground, but here and there, it is beginning to melt. The hamster comes up from his burrow to take a quick look around.

In the farmer's field, a few stalks remain from the rich wheat harvest of autumn. The hamster also had a good harvest last year. Throughout the summer, he collected grains of wheat and stuffed them into his cheek pouches. Then he took his collection down into the storeroom of his burrow. The hamster also gathered sunflower seeds, grains of rye, and kernels of corn for his winter food supply.

Some foods—juicy plums, for example—the hamster ate right on the spot. After every meal, he would clean his snout and whiskers thoroughly with his front paws. Cleanliness is very important to him, as it is to all hamsters. In his burrow, he even has a special bathroom area next to his sleeping quarters and storeroom.

When winter came, the hamster curled up in his bedroom and went to sleep. Every five days or so, he woke up and got something to eat from his food supply.

Now, after his look around on this late winter day, the hamster decides that winter is not quite over. He goes back into his burrow for one more nap before spring.

Scientific name: *Cricetus cricetus*
Body length: 11 inches (30 cm)
Weight: About 1 pound (500 g)
Food: Grain, corn, sunflower seeds, fruits, snails, worms
Lifespan: 2½ years

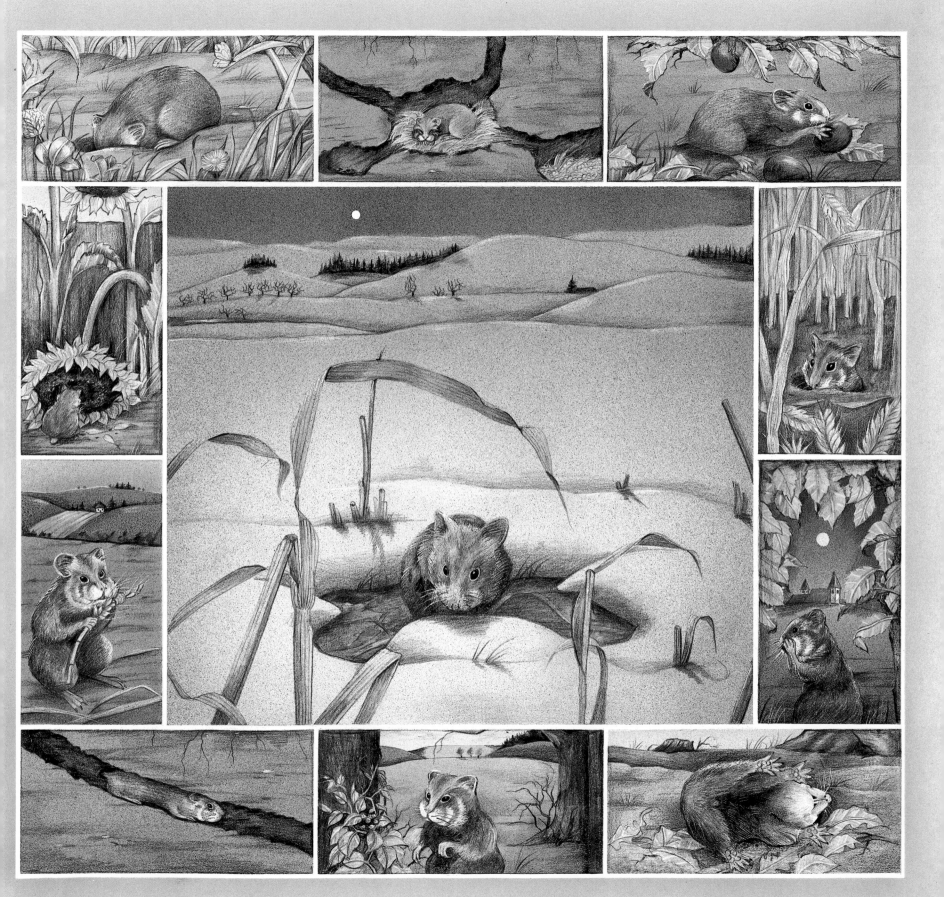

BRIMSTONE BUTTERFLY

At last, the cold season is over. The winter months were hard for the brimstone butterfly. Stiff and cold, he lay hidden in leaves under the snow. A special substance in his blood helped to prevent his body from freezing. But this winter was especially cold, and many butterflies did not survive.

Now it is spring, and the butterfly flutters over the sweet-smelling meadow. He visits bluebells and blooming fruit trees, sucking nectar from the flowers.

In summer, the brimstone butterfly will mate with a female of his species. She will lay her eggs on a buckthorn bush, and soon a little green caterpillar will emerge from every egg. The caterpillars will eat the buckthorn leaves and grow larger until it is time for them to go through the next big change in their lives. Attached to stems by silken threads, they will become pupae. About a week later, the pupal shells will break open, and out will come new brimstone butterflies.

Scientific name: *Gonepteryx rhamni*
Wingspan: 2 inches (5.5 cm)
Food: Nectar, juice from ripe fruit
Lifespan: 1 year

The butterflies will try their new wings during the cool autumn days. When winter comes, they too will hide themselves away and wait for spring.

AMERICAN ANIMALS IN WINTER

Several kinds of **marmots** live in the mountains of western North America. They are very much like the marmot described in this book. The groundhog, or woodchuck (*Marmota monax*), is a marmot from the eastern part of North America. Groundhogs are supposed to forecast the end of winter by coming out of hibernation in February.

Snails related to the European garden (or edible) snail are found in many parts of the world, including North America. These snails often hibernate in winter and also go through a period of inactivity during the hot, dry summer.

The **American badger** (*Taxidea taxus*) has different markings than the European badger, but the two animals are close relatives. Many European and American badgers remain active during the winter. Only in very cold regions do the animals hibernate.

The **hazel mouse** is a kind of dormouse, a small rodent that has a hairy tail and lives in trees. Dormice are not found in North America, but some American mice such as the jumping mouse (*Zapus hudsonius*) are hibernators.

Many relatives of the **common European frog** live in North America. Among them are the leopard frog (*Rana pipiens*) and the green frog (*Rana clamitans*). All frogs that live in areas with cold winters hibernate.

The **little brown bat** of North America is a close relative of the European mouse-eared bat and has similar habits. Both belong to the scientific group called *Myotis*.

Hedgehogs live only in Europe and Asia. The porcupine is an American animal with a spiny coat, but it is not closely related to the hedgehog. The porcupine is a rodent like the beaver, while the hedgehog's relatives are moles, shrews, and other insect-eaters.

The North American **red squirrel** (*Tamiasciurus hudsonicus*) usually has smaller ear tufts than its European cousin, but its habits are similar. Both squirrels are active during the winter, staying in their nests only during very bad weather.

The **fat dormouse** is another well-known European animal that does not live in North America. Many Americans are probably familiar with at least one dormouse— the sleepy one that comes to the Mad Hatter's tea party in *Alice in Wonderland*.

There are several kinds of **brown bears** found in North America. The grizzly bear and the Kodiak bear of Alaska are both members of this group (*Ursus arctos*). All brown bears are hibernators.

The **European hamster** is a close relative of the golden hamster (*Mesocricetus auratus*), which people often keep as a pet. No wild hamsters live in North America.

The **brimstone butterfly** is a member of a large family of butterflies common in North America. The cabbage butterfly (*Pieris rapae*) and the orange-tip butterfly (*Anthocharis cardamines*) belong to this group. The brimstone butterfly has a much longer life span than most of its relatives. Many butterflies live only a few days or weeks after they become adults.

nic